the Way
of the
Warrior

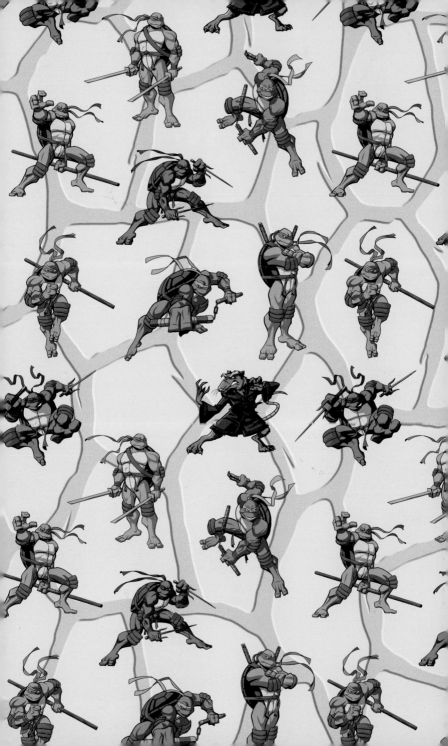

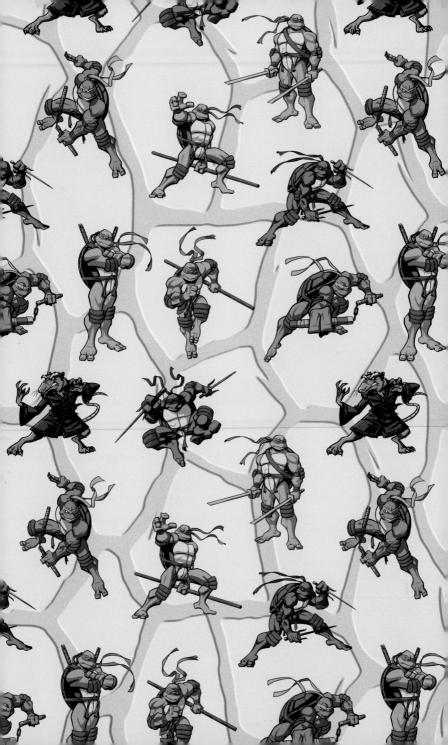

First published in hardback in Great Britain by HarperCollins Publishers Ltd in 2003

First published in paperback in Great Britain by HarperCollins Publishers Ltd in 2003

1 3 5 7 9 10 8 6 4 2

ISBN: 0-00-717900-6

Printed and bound in Hong Kong

the Way
of the
Warrior

An imprint of HarperCollins*Publishers*

Konnishiha, future warriors! I am Master Splinter, wise sensei. You have much to learn about your ninja destiny and it is my pleasure to teach you. To survive, you must master these skills I teach you... Ninjitsu powers of stealth and secrecy. You must become kage! Shadow warriors!

Join me, Leonardo, Raphael, Michelangelo and Donatello and prepare to discover...

the Way
of the
Warrior.

Contents

In the beginning...

My tale begins with four tiny turtles and a canister of green slime. I saw the little creatures collide with the canister and spill into the sewer. They were covered with the strange glowing goo. I had to rescue them!

The turtles began to grow quickly, but also to change. To mutate! In the twisting sewer system deep beneath the city streets I raised my new family, teaching them all I knew about the ancient art of ninjitsu – the ninja warrior ways.

I named them Leonardo, Raphael, Michelangelo, Donatello – together they have bonded into a supreme green fighting team, Teenage Mutant Ninja Turtles! Now they are ready to battle all that is evil in the world. And of that there is much, my friends, as you are soon to find out…

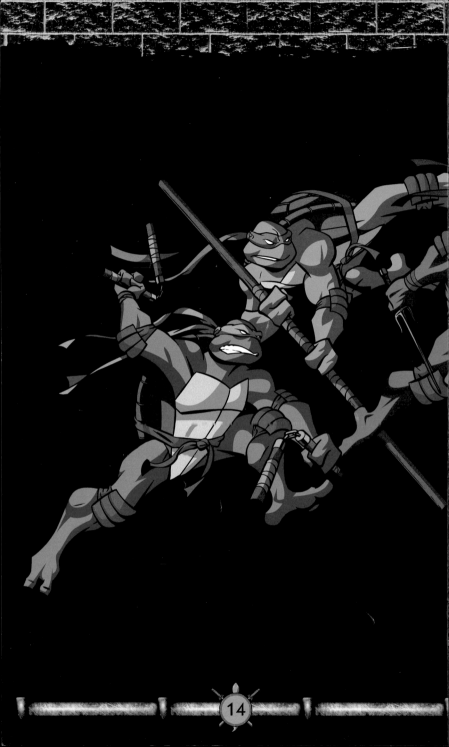

Meet the Turtles...

Leonardo™
dedicated, disciplined and selfless

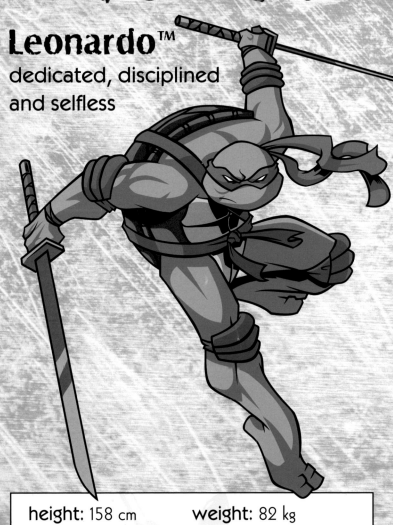

height: 158 cm   **weight:** 82 kg

age: 15

weapon: twin katana swords to match his sharp mind and steely resolve

nicknames: Leo, Fearless Leader

likes: candles

hobby: ninjitsu training — no time for anything else!

food: pizza! Also rice, fish and salads

colour: blue

music: traditional Japanese

time: when they all sit together at dinner and listen to Splinter's stories and teachings

Leonardo is a way cool hero. Dedicated to his brothers and sensei, Master Splinter, ninjitsu is his life. No one trains harder than Leo! Serious and responsible, he's the big brother of the group and unofficial leader. He sometimes loses patience if the others are goofing around too much, but when it's fight time Leo's brilliant battle strategies mean the Turtles can really kick butt!

most likely to say: Teamwork equals success

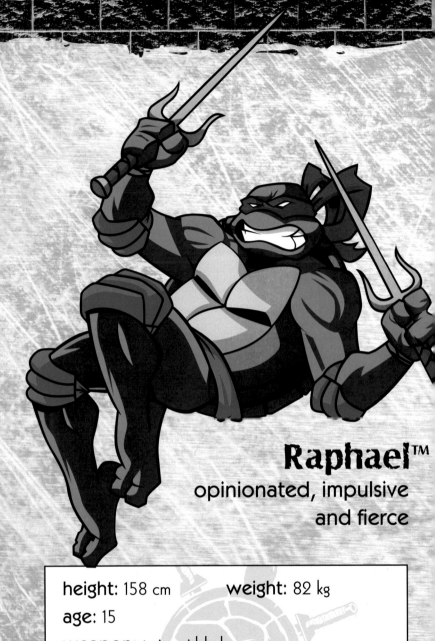

Raphael™
opinionated, impulsive and fierce

height: 158 cm   **weight:** 82 kg

age: 15

weapon: twin sai blades

nicknames: Raph, Raphie, Psycho, Secret Weapon

likes: sneakin' off to the Topside and street ridin' with Casey

hobbies: baseball, hockey, golf and fighting!

food: cereal

colour: red

music: punk, rap, metal — it's gotta be loud!

time: when it's time to apply some Turtle whacks!

Raphie is a hothead and then some. He practises his battle skills for total enjoyment and is the most confident Ninja Turtle of the group. Restless and always ready for battle, he's usually first into the fight. If the guys are outnumbered then that's even better — giving up is just not Raph, right?

most likely to say: Alrighty then… who wants some?!

Michelangelo™

flamboyant, flashy
and fearless

height: 158 cm   weight: 82 kg

age: 15

weapon: nunchaku

nickname: Mikey
likes: fun, fun, FUN!
hobbies: music, surfing, skating, playing computer games and reading comics
food: pizza!
colour: orange
music: rap, techno and surf music
time: party time!

Mikey is a party lovin' dude. Flashy and fun, he's the joker of the group. Ninja training isn't always top of his list but Mike's strength makes up for his lack of interest in his lessons. Mike loves music, film, TV and video which makes him your guy for all things entertainment. His clowning around can drive his brothers mad, but he just thinks they need to chill, man!

most likely to say: Happiness is a journey, not a destination — let's party, dudes!

Donatello™

courageous,
inspired and
intelligent

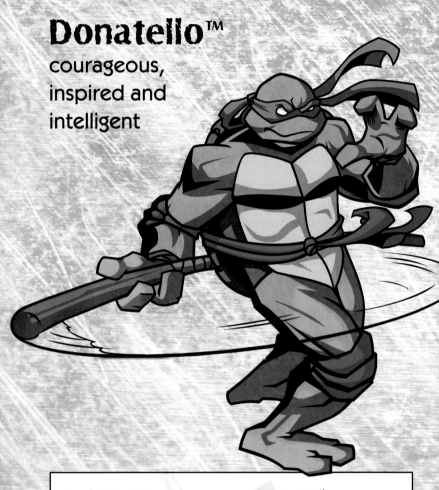

height: 158 cm   **weight:** 82 kg

age: 15

weapon: bo staff – long on inspiration and
stout of heart

nicknames: Don, Donny, Don –San

likes: inventing cool stuff

hobbies: maths, science, engineering, computers

food: pizza! And sushi

colour: purple

music: classical

time: when he's busy working in his laboratory or scouring Smitty's junkyard

Nobody knows how he does it (not even him!), but Donatello is the techie of the group. Need an escape – mobile, communication device or trick shuriken? Don's your guy. Inventor of all the Turtles' funky vehicles and lotsa super-handy gadgets, he's a green genius. More peace-loving and quiet than the others, but he can still give those baddies some shell!

most likely to say: Unless I've grossly miscalculated, we're about to get our biscuits beaten!

Which Turtle Are You?

Pick one thing from each list to find out
which of the green guys you're most like.

M L R D
III IIII I II
III III IIII

Choose a colour...

Orange	☑	M
Blue	☐	L
Red	☒	R
Purple	☐	D

What's your dream job?

Astronaut	☒	D
Formula 1 racing driver	☐	R
Movie stuntman	☐	M
World leader	☑	L

Your fave school subject is...

Maths and science	☐	D
English or languages	☐	L
Art and design	☐	M
Sports	☒	R

Rate your homework happiness out of 10...

2 – yawn! Homework is sooo Dullsville ☐ R

6 – ok, but you've got better things to do ☐ M

8 – it's always cool to learn new things ☐ D

9 – study and knowledge are important ☒ L

Pick a hobby...

Skating ☒ M

BMX biking ☒ R

Reading ☐ L

Computer games ☐ D

Your room is...

Super tidy and organised ☒ L

Soo messy you can't remember what colour the carpet is ☐ M

Alright – you're too busy to spend much time there ☐ R

Pretty untidy, but it's all way important stuff ☐ D

You'd rather watch...

An action movie ☐ R

A science fiction movie ☒ D

Super-hero stories ☐ L

Cartoons ☐ M

Pick a fave sport

Footie ☑ L
WWA ☐ R
Basketball ☒ D
Athletics ☐ M

If you could go anywhere in the world you'd choose...

Italy ☐ R
Japan ☐ L
UK ☐ M
USA ☑ D

Which super-hero power would you most love to have?

Be invisible ☒ L
Change shape ☐ D
Be able to fly ☑ M
Super strength ☐ R

Conclusions

Mostly L

You are Leonardo — dependable, trustworthy and loyal. If you need a plan, you da guy! You make a great mate and always do what you say you will. Organised and never late, you can get annoyed if others aren't always on time. Don't forget that it's also cool to relax and chill. You can be a bit too serious and there's plenty of time for that when you're older, man!

Mostly R

Wow! Cross you and sparks will fly! You've got a way fiery temper, just like Raphael. If something gets you going you don't even stop to think, you just jump right on in. Although you're really kind-hearted and would do anything for a pal, your fierceness can put some people off. Next time you feel like losin' it, try to count to 10 and calm down a bit FIRST.

Mostly D

Just like Donatello, you're happiest when you've got something to build, make or do. You know lots about lots and you get inspiration from all over. Sometimes you can appear a bit geeky, but your mates know the real deal. Your funky ideas are mondo cool and they know who to turn to for the best gadget-tastic gang hut in the land.

Mostly M

Hey, were you and Mikey separated at birth? You love to joke and party to the max — though sometimes joking in the wrong place (like class!) can get you into big trouble. Always running late and totally disorganised, but loveable with it! You're happiest chillin' with your friends, watching movies or with your head stuck in a comic.

Friends...

Even butt-kickin' Ninja Turtles need a hand now and then. The first battle is to pick a great mate and hang on to them. We know we can always rely on our friends, April and Casey.

As Master Splinter would say, "A friend is one who knows who you are, understands where you have been, accepts what you have become and still gently invites you to grow. Goodness and evil are choices. So choose wisely."

Yeah, and Master Mikey would say something a whole lot simpler like, "A problem shared is a problem halved!"

Serious Butt-kickin'
Ninja Puzzles!

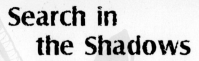

Search in the Shadows

Use your ninja skills to find these words hidden in the shadows.

Words can read forwards, backwards, up, down or diagonally. Letters can be used more than once.

TURTLE	GREEN
DOJO	LEONARDO
DONATELLO	MICHELANGELO
RAPHAEL	SPLINTER
NINJA	SHREDDER
APRIL	CASEY
LAIR	SEWER
WAREHOUSE	BO STAFF
SAI	NUNCHAKU
KATANAS	SEWERSLIDER
SHELLCYCLE	RAILRACER
BATTLEWAGON	SHELLCELL

V	R	V	Q	E	G	O	M	Q	I	R	L
R	R	I	H	W	O	R	V	W	A	K	L
S	A	N	A	T	A	K	E	P	S	F	E
H	M	S	R	L	G	T	H	E	O	K	C
J	R	Y	H	G	U	A	R	X	N	X	L
M	Y	Z	B	R	E	B	I	Z	D	Y	L
B	A	T	T	L	E	W	A	G	O	N	E
S	R	F	E	B	A	D	O	V	D	S	H
G	E	X	F	J	Q	D	D	O	W	H	S
R	A	W	N	A	R	K	N	E	S	E	O
C	E	I	E	A	T	A	G	E	R	L	N
U	N	C	N	R	T	S	W	T	E	L	U
W	N	O	O	E	S	E	O	G	O	C	N
E	E	A	L	R	R	L	N	B	C	Y	C
L	P	L	T	Y	L	A	I	X	A	C	H
T	O	J	O	D	L	I	B	D	S	L	A
R	P	A	D	E	I	E	A	M	E	E	K
U	H	I	H	X	G	P	Y	R	Y	R	U
T	P	C	E	S	U	O	H	E	R	A	W
U	I	I	S	P	L	I	N	T	E	R	A
M	Y	E	A	P	R	I	L	D	Z	C	Z

Hidden Treasure

Tch! Wait till I get my hands on
that pesky Michelangelo! He's sooo
going to see some serious butt-kickin'
ninja action.

Mikey has hidden my sai and left me a list of
clues on where to find 'em. Help me fill in the answers
and the hiding place will appear in the shaded area.

Clues:

1. This is what we are

2. A shadow warrior

3. Area where ninja training takes place

4. A very, very bad thing

5. We're this colour

6. Don's fave junkyard

7. Casey's surname

8. Baxter Stockman's evil invention

9. It's short for Raphael

10. Don's weapon

11. Master Splinter is a wise one

12. Another name for Oroku Saki

TURTLES

1.
2.
3.
4.
5.
6.
7.
8.
9.
10.
11.
12.

Sounds Cool

Hey you guys, how much do
you love music? I'm always
wired for sound. Solve these
puzzles to find out what's spinin'
on my stereo right now.

Cross out the letters that appear 3 times
or more in each box to reveal some cool sounds.

B	H	L	W	B	U	D
W	E	N	I	U	E	B
B	N	W	D	Y	P	M
L	Y	H	M	E	N	Y
M	O	W	L	D	U	P

R	E	E	O	F
D	Y	D	H	E
Y	C	F	Y	H
H	F	Y	K	D

H	P	O	E	C	A
C	U	P	B	V	O
B	O	Z	Y	M	Z
U	Z	E	T	P	P
B	C	U	B	A	L

Short Circuit

I've been working real hard on
a funky new gadget. It's wicked!
Solve the alphabet clues
and find out what it is.

1. Go to the 12th letter of the alphabet and
   count back 9

2. Go to the letter that comes before K and
   count forward 5

3. Divide 14 by 2 then subtract 3.
   Choose that letter of the alphabet.

4. What's the square root of 25? Pick that letter.

5. It's the letter that comes before N.

6. The opposite of the last letter of the alphabet.

7. Subtract 4 from 26 then divide by 2.
   Pick that letter.

8. Get this letter by adding 5 + 5 + 5 then
   dividing by 3.

9. The letter after Q.

Write your answers in here...

1	2	3	4	5	6	7	8	9

Sewer Run

My sons, your shadow warrior skills are needed to battle evil. Hurry through the sewers to meet me in the dojo.

Enemies...

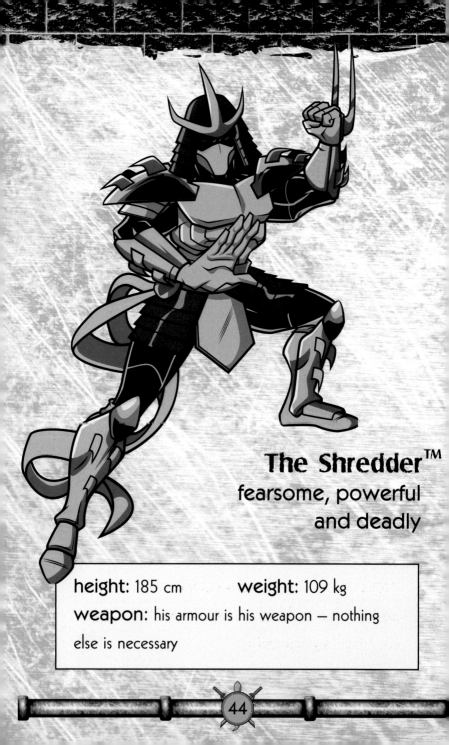

The Shredder™
fearsome, powerful and deadly

height: 185 cm   **weight:** 109 kg

weapon: his armour is his weapon — nothing else is necessary

nickname: no one would dare give him a nickname

likes: winning!

hobbies: conquering the world

food: food is of no importance

colour: red – the colour of blood

music: Shredder has no time for such foolishness

time: the time when he becomes ruler of all things

Who would guess that Oroku Saki, wealthy and respected Japanese nobleman, is the fearsome Shredder? He is Master of the dreaded Foot clan, an ancient ninja order. One of the world's most skilled ninjitsu warriors, he has twisted the teachings for his own evil ends. The Shredder cares for no one and thinks nothing of crushing those who cross him – even his own elite force.

most likely to say: Bow before my magnificence and might, o worm, and I may spare you when my time arrives.

The Foot
physical, psychological and mystical

The Foot

The Foot have existed for many centuries, ruthless shadow warriors moving through the global underworld. They have closely studied the ways of the ninja to become a successful criminal group and have a network of dangerous divisions. Cross them at your peril!

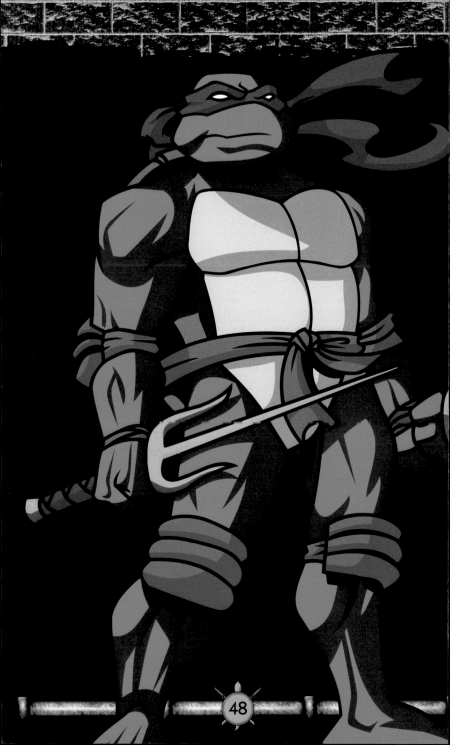

Talk Turtle!

Hey guys, wanna talk Turtle?
Get with the green, it's way past cool!

IT'S SO EASY BEING GREEN

TURTLE-IZE 'EM

TIME TO APPLY SOME TURTLE WHACKS!

BANZAI!

Guide To Ninja Wisdom...

Nothing comes from outside your mind...

Gashi, my noble students.

Entering the world of the ninja is a wise choice.
The ancient ninjitsu teachings have many seeds
of wisdom. The words can have many meanings,
some which may seem at odds with what you
already know. Study them well with patience
and care and their true light will shine through.
One drop of ink may make a million think.

The violent will not come to a natural end

You must see both sides to understand the whole

Evil is hard to hide, look for it on the face of your enemy

Beware the treachery that lurks in your enemy's heart

Advice is what we ask for when we already know the answer but wish we didn't

Better a diamond with a flaw than a pebble without one (something I often think about my dear but hotheaded Raphael)

Learning is a treasure that will follow its owner everywhere

A fair face may fade, but a beautiful soul lasts forever

Concentration of thought and focus of energy yield power

Turn the energy of your emotions to your favour

Obsession is dedication out of control

Action may not always be happiness, but there is no happiness without action

An angry person is seldom reasonable; a reasonable person is seldom angry

All sunshine makes a desert

You cannot prevent the birds of sorrow from flying over your head, but you can prevent them from nesting in your hair

Practise your moves very slowly to execute them with great speed

Your weapons are an extension of you – match them to your needs

Know Your
Ninja Destiny

Learning the ways of the ninja is a long journey in life. To be a true ninja master takes many years. Before starting out on this road I ask all of my students what they hope to learn and achieve through the teachings. These questions will help you discover your true ninja destiny.

1. Which of these animals would you most like to be?

A   giant panda

B   lion

C   elephant

2. Two of your best friends have fallen out, do you...

B   take sides with one of them and refuse to speak to the other?

A   try to stay friends with both of them, but it's really not your fight?

C   get them together and try to talk things through?

3. Which of these would you rather do?

B   go to an adventure park with lots of your pals

A   go 10 pin bowling with your best friend

C   practise some cool moves at the local skate park

4. Your best friend has borrowed your fave CD. When you get it back it's too scratched to play. What do you do?

C   you're sad that he didn't tell you about it and you say this to him. A problem between friends can always be fixed.

B   fly into a temper, shout at him for 20 minutes and vow never to speak to him again.

A   say nothing. If it ever happens again you'll discuss it with him. It was probably an accident anyway.

5. Your best mate's birthday party is on the same day as your gran's birthday tea. What do you do?

B   stomp, huff and stay in a deeply bad mood all day

A   ask your mate if there's anyway he can change the day of his party

C   apologise for not being able to go to the party but arrange to do something special with your friend really soon

6. You have broken your mum's favourite vase whilst practising your ninja moves. Do you...

C   own up straight away and offer to buy another one with your pocket money?

B   glue it back together and hope she doesn't notice?

A   apologise and give her a big hug?

Conclusions

Mostly A – Peacelover

You like to think carefully before taking any action. No rushing in feet first for you. If you can, you prefer to sort things out by talking rather than fighting, though sometimes you say nothing at all to avoid confrontation. But you are honest and honorable and friends can trust you to always tell the truth.

Mostly B – Warrior

Brave and fearless, you have mastered the secret ways of the shadow warrior well and are never slow to join the fight. Sometimes this can be a bit foolish as force is not always the best way. Try to think about each situation before your hot head takes over. Friends can always depend on you to stand by them.

Mostly C - Wise Sensei

You have the patience and skills to instruct others in the ancient teachings of the ninja. You have studied both the warrior ways and the wise words of life carefully. Passing this information to others is your destiny. Your ability to see both sides means you are good at sorting out arguments between others. Friends will turn to you for help and advice.

More Turtle Teachings...

Leo's Ninjitsu Dictionary

aite – opponent

battojutsu – sword-drawing techniques

bikenjutsu – swords-turtleship

budoka – one who studies the martial ways

bujin – warrior spirit

chunin – historically, a mid-level ninja
(genin is low-level and jonin is higer-level)

dojo – training hall

genjutsu – arts of illusion

heiho – military strategy

inpo – the art of hiding

inton – camouflage and concealment

ninja – shadow warrior

ninja juhachikei – 18 levels of ninja training

ninpo – the higher order of ninjutsu

o sensei – great teacher

shinobi ho – the art of stealth

shinobi juhappan – 18 ninja skills

yamikeigo – ninja practice in the dark

Count Down in Japanese with Raphael

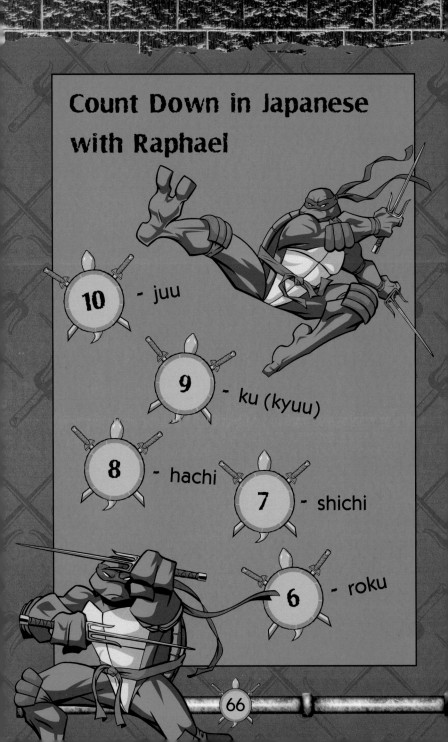

10 - juu

9 - ku (kyuu)

8 - hachi

7 - shichi

6 - roku

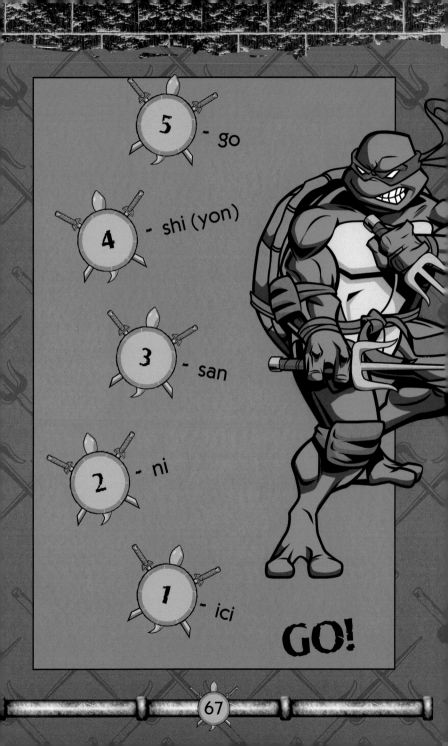

5 - go

4 - shi (yon)

3 - san

2 - ni

1 - ici

GO!

Things You Didn't Know About Mikey

…Mike taught himself to play guitar. Not that easy when you've only got 3 fingers!

…Michelangelo loves doodling and often sketches out his own super-hero characters.

…Mike's best bud is Raph. His jokey sense of humour is often the only thing that can get Raphael out of a rage.

…he's the most imaginative of all the Turtles. Earth calling Fantasy Mikey Land!

…he loves to skate across the rooftops of New York City. Shellacious!

…his fave vehicle is the Sewer Slider. Totally butt-kickin'!

Check Out Don's Invention Checklist!

ShellCell Communication Device:
Mobile phone Turtle-style! This funky little number even has a video cam and screen. Cool!

Night Vision Goggles:
Sometimes even the best Turtles can't see too great in the shadows. These guys sort that prob, pronto. With a ShellCell headset to stay connected they're wicked.

Trick Shuriken:
Looks like plain and simple throwing blades, but these babies aren't quite what they seem!

Laboratory
It's all goin' on in here!

My days as a ninja warrior are reaching an end as time passes too quickly for my old bones. I must seek a new path, that of scholar, and I spend much of my time in meditation and the quiet contemplation of life. It is always in season for old men to learn.

Some call me Master, but I have yet to fully embrace the true power of ninjitsu. Very few indeed are able to learn and understand all the teachings. The perceptions are ever-changing. My studies and practise continue and, meanwhile, I must pass on what I do know to my sons.

In an ideal world we could conquer evil with peaceful means, but sadly this is not so. The force of evil is only as strong as your willingness to surrender to it and I will never give in. However, do not forget that great care must be taken in the routes we choose – never sacrifice honor for victory.

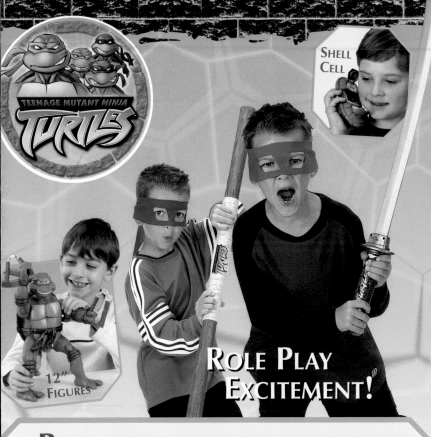
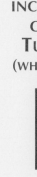

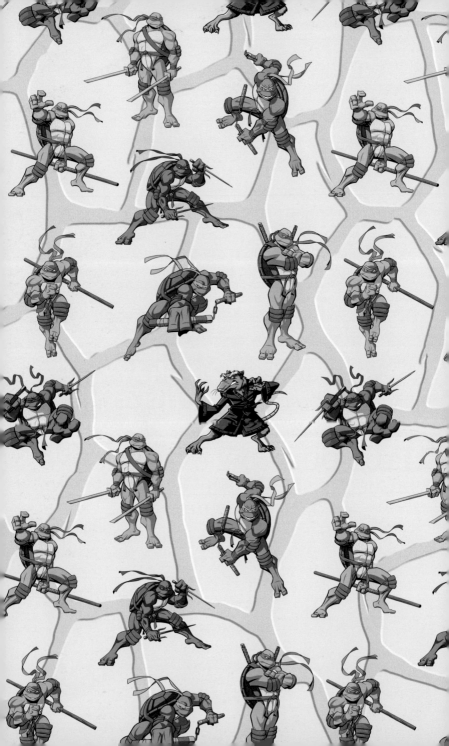